Carving & P... RED-TAILED HAWK *with Floyd Scholz*

Curtis J. Badger

STACKPOLE BOOKS

Published by
STACKPOLE BOOKS
5067 Ritter Road
Mechanicsburg, PA 17055

Printed in Hong Kong

10 9 8 7 6 5 4 3 2 1

First edition

All photographs by the author unless otherwise credited.

Library of Congress Cataloging-in-Publication Data

Badger, Curtis J.
    Carving and painting a red-tailed hawk with Floyd Scholz /
  Curtis J. Badger. — 1st ed.
      p.   cm.
    ISBN 0-8117-2704-1
    1. Scholz, Floyd—Themes, motives. 2. Wood-carving—
Technique. 3. Painting—Technique. 4. Red-tailed hawk in art.
I. Scholz, Floyd. II. Title.
NK9798.S36A4   1997
730'.92—dc21   97-2486
                                     CIP

Contents

CHAPTER ONE

Floyd Scholz— Enamored of Raptors

Floyd Scholz's work is imbued with the history and natural history of Vermont. His studio is in a village landmark—an eighteenth-century one-room schoolhouse that sits alongside the Hancock Branch of the White River. It's here that Floyd devotes countless hours to studying, carving, and painting the raptors that patrol the green hillsides and fields of the Green Mountains surrounding this quiet part of Vermont.

He lives in Hancock, a neat little village about an hour south of Burlington. Hancock is on the White River, on the eastern margin of the Green Mountains. Much of the land around Hancock is included in the Green Mountain National Forest, and other tracts are protected by the state or by private conservation groups such as the Nature Conservancy.

A national survey recently found that Vermont is the safest state in the country, and a subsequent regional survey found that Addison County, which includes Hancock, is the safest in Vermont. Visiting Hancock is like stepping into a movie set from the 1940s. All the homes look freshly painted, the lawns are nicely manicured, the people are friendly, and the kids probably score above average on their college entrance exams. People in Hancock don't lock their doors at night, an anomaly in America these days. There is no police department; there wouldn't be enough business to keep one busy.

Hancock's one-room school-house has been filled with students from the time it was built in 1806 until 1990. Just two decades ago, the student population ranged from grade one through high school. In the 1970s, the high schoolers were sent to a consolidated regional school, and finally, in 1990, the school doors were closed altogether. The building remained vacant until 1996, when the village decided to sell. Floyd had been using a rather cramped studio in a barn loft in town and had been teaching seminars around the country for several years. When he learned that the old schoolhouse was for sale, he quickly bought it, made some needed renovations, moved in his tools and equipment, and set up a classroom space. Today classes are once again in session at the one-room schoolhouse, as carvers come from around the country to study with Floyd and other top carvers at the Vermont Raptor Academy.

Floyd was an outstanding track athlete in college, a two-time All-American in the demanding decathlon. Thoughts of Olympic fame and lucrative endorsements occurred to him, but a career-ending hamstring injury while participating in the NCAA Championships ended those dreams.

Floyd Scholz is not exactly a believer in mysticism, but he has a strong suspicion that his life has a certain predetermined direction and that events along the way are designed to nudge him in that direction, even if they are at times painful. So he has no remorse at missing out on the fame and endorsement checks. "I was beginning to burn out," he says. "I was probably in the top 10 percent in this country in the decathlon, but when it came to international competition, that was another story. I refused to take steroids, and at the time it was hard to get to the top in international track without them."

Floyd moved to Hancock in 1980 after graduating from Central Connecticut State University with a degree in industrial education and some rather ambiguous plans for the future. He was interested in mountain hiking, birds of prey, working with wood, and learning to play the banjo. He wasn't sure how those ingredients would fit together in the form of a career, but the Green Mountains of Vermont seemed a good place to sit back and let life simmer while things sorted themselves out.

He had originally intended to teach school, but he found that logging paid better and the physical labor was therapeutic. He later worked for a building contractor, then bought his own piece of Vermont, a 55-acre farm in the North Hollow, just outside Hancock. In 1983, he began carving full-time. Eventually, Floyd's skill at bird carving made the other jobs unnecessary, and he has managed to combine his love of mountains, raptors, and wood to become one of the world's leading wildfowl sculptors. He is a recognized master at capturing the beauty and drama of birds of prey, and his carved birds are in the most prominent private collections and museums. And he has learned to play not only the banjo, but blues guitar as well.

In 1990, Floyd fell in love with and married a woman from Venezuela whom he had met in town, and they settled into a spacious home overlooking Hancock and the Green Mountain National Forest. Each morning he drives down the mountain to the little one-room schoolhouse, where he goes to work.

Floyd has developed a reputation as the raptor man of Vermont. He carves several songbirds each year but is known primarily for his eagles, hawks, and other large birds of prey. Since he began carving full-time, he has collected some twenty-six best-in-show ribbons in art competitions around the country. His work has been shown in numerous wildlife art museums, including the prestigious Leigh Yawkey Woodson in Wausau, Wisconsin.

Floyd enjoys the drama, grace, and mystery of birds of prey. He has spent thousands of hours observing hawks and eagles in the mountains near his home, and he has watched them as they interact with their environment, playing in the wind above the cliffs of nearby Mount Horrid and hunting in the spruce thickets along the White River.

"I think birds of prey appeal to something in all of us," he says. "They're predators; they're at the top of the food chain; they're fearless. I like their look, their attitude, their independence and integrity. Humans throughout history have been fascinated with birds of prey, especially eagles and hawks. Indian tribes worshiped them. Genghis Khan rode into battle with a golden eagle on his fist. They're strong, agile, incredible fliers. They symbolize qualities I feel are important."

Floyd studied birds of prey intently for several years while working as a volunteer for the Peregrine Fund, which at the time was based at Cornell University in New York. "The Peregrine Fund was begun by Dr. Tom Cade in an attempt to reestablish peregrines along traditional East Coast habitat," he says. "I helped out from around 1982 to 1985 when they released captive-bred peregrines on Mount Horrid in central Vermont. It was a great experience, spending a lot of time on the mountain and becoming friends with so many experts. The things I learned about birds—anatomy and attitude and so forth—provided a great foundation for the work I was doing in the studio. It's a good feeling to have a peregrine expert come by and look at a bird I'm sculpting and offer a critique. In wildfowl art, you have to spend a lot of time in the field looking at birds and getting ideas. I'll hike up Mount Horrid, sit on the cliffs, and watch the birds play around in the wind. That's how I got the idea for the golden eagle I did recently. I even brought back a sample of rock so I could duplicate it in wood."

Floyd carved his first bird, a miniature mallard drake, at age ten. As with many wildfowl artists, an interest in birds and artistic talent ran on parallel tracks, which inevitably converged. In Floyd's case, the connection between birds and art was brought home by his uncle, George Csefai, who had fled communist oppression in Hungary in 1956 and settled in Connecticut. George was a gifted carver whose life was tragically shortened by cancer, and although he died when Floyd was ten, he had a profound influence on Floyd's life.

"George married my aunt Donna and brought much to the family," says Floyd. "He was a vibrant, talented man, an incredible athlete, an avid outdoorsman. He was a machinist and could make anything. He won many of the early carving competitions and before he became ill was thinking of becoming a full-time carver. He's the one who got me interested in doing birds. I saw the things he was doing, and I thought it was pure magic."

Although his uncle sparked his interest in sculpting birds, Floyd learned the technical aspects of carving on his own. "When I was growing up in Connecticut, I was working in isolation as far as wildfowl art is concerned," he says. "What I've learned I picked up on my own. There were no courses at the local schools and no other carvers in the neighborhood to study with. I got Bruce Burk's *Game Bird Carving,* and picked up some fundamentals there, but most of the carving techniques I learned by trial and error. When I started going to exhibitions, I met and developed a deep friendship with John Scheeler, who helped me a lot. And to this day his influences come forth in my work. I guess I learned a little from everyone. What drew me to John's work were the stories he would convey through his pieces: the predator-prey struggle, the conviction of a peregrine falcon sitting on a rock, the elegance of a preening heron."

Not coincidentally, Floyd's sculptures of birds of prey also have this narrative sense, this effect of a bird caught in freeze-frame during some particularly revealing moment, like a Cartier-Bresson photograph. This quality is impossible to learn in the classroom or the carving seminar. In Floyd's case, his best teacher has probably been the mountains of Vermont. You can learn the technical aspects of wood sculpture anywhere, but you have to spend time with the birds to be able to capture in art a decisive moment in the life of a raptor. The watching and learning seem as important to Floyd as the hours in the studio, and it's not just the birds that matter, but also something vital Floyd has found in the land and the community here.

"Whenever I've been away for a while and come back to this valley, it's like stepping back from the edge. I feel secure here. It's womblike. I want to spend the rest of my life here, and when my time comes to go, I'd like to be in my schoolhouse hard at work on my next carving."

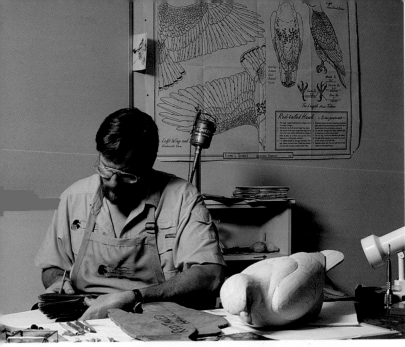

Floyd at work in his one-room schoolhouse in Hancock, Vermont.

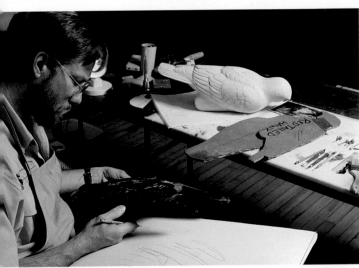

Good reference material is vital to ensure accuracy. Here Floyd studies the wing of a mounted bird as he works on the carving of the hawk.

Floyd has lived in Hancock since graduating from college. Here he holds one of his hawks in progress.

CHAPTER TWO

About the Red-tailed Hawk

The cry of a red-tailed hawk is not something one soon forgets. In the quiet countryside, with only a gentle breeze rustling the trees, it is a piercing sound, like the shriek of a small animal caught in mortal peril.

The red-tail screams as it hunts, soaring and drifting over open fields and woodlands. I don't know why it screams, but I suspect it has something to do with luring small mammals into the open, perhaps to see what possible misfortune might have befallen one of their own. Small mammals perhaps are, like humans, ambulance chasers. We slow down when approaching highway accidents, watching with a combination of fascination and concern. Perhaps small animals are like that, a rabbit responding to a rabbitlike scream with fascination and curiosity, until it is tricked into becoming a meal.

Red-tailed hawks have great visual power, and they hunt as they glide or perch in tall trees, scanning the fields and woods for mice, voles, rabbits, squirrels, chipmunks, and other small animals. When they spot a possible victim, they go into a quiet and shallow dive, striking the target with sharp talons. The red-tail is one of our largest buteos, a strong, stocky bird that can easily take out a small animal simply by blunt force—a 3-pound guided missile armed with razor wire.

The taxonomic name of the red-tail is *Buteo jamaicensis*, the genus being Latin for hawk and the species referring to Jamaica, the island in the West Indies where the first specimens were found. The red-tail is North America's most widespread hawk, a resident of or regular visitor to all of the continental United States and most of the Canadian provinces. Shortly after World War II, the population of red-tails dropped sharply in North America, mainly because of predation by humans, who considered the big hawk a killer of barnyard fowl, game birds, and even house pets. Pesticides that hampered the birds' reproductive success took their toll, as they also did on eagles, ospreys, and other large birds near the top of the food chain. But today the populations of red-tails and many other hawks are healthy, thanks to a more enlightened attitude among humans, stricter legal protection, and a ban on harmful pesticides.

As with most hawks, the female red-tail is larger than the male. John Terres, in the *Audubon Society Encyclopedia of North American Birds,* gives the weight of the males as 2 pounds, 4 ounces to 2 pounds, 8 ounces. The female weighs 3 pounds to 3 pounds, 8 ounces. The birds are 19 to 25 inches long, with a wingspread of 46 to 58 inches.

Red-tails, like all buteos, are built for slow, sustained flight, with a thick body, wide wings, and a broad tail. They are gliders and soarers rather than speed merchants like peregrines and other falcons, yet they can cruise at level flight at 35 to 40 miles per hour and are capable of 120 miles per hour in a dive.

Carving and painting a red-tail presents an interesting array of choices to the artist. Will the bird be male or female? Mature or immature? Dark or light phase? The red-tailed hawk varies widely in color characteristics. In the East, most red-tails are dark brown above, white below, with a broad, broken dark band across the belly. Adults have brown eyes, yellow lores, and chestnut red on the upper side of the tail. Immatures have yellow eyes and significantly more mottling on the dark upperparts.

A Great Plains subspecies, Krider's hawk, has paler upperparts and a light red tail. Most southwestern red-tails lack the dark belly band of the eastern birds. And another subspecies, Harlan's hawk, once considered a separate species, is a darker bird with a dusky white tail. To further complicate things, some red-tails, primarily those in the West, have a dark, or melanistic, phase. These birds have dark wing linings and underparts, and the tail is dark red above.

So when planning a carving and painting project whose subject is a red-tailed hawk, judicious research is called for, as well as some decision making. The bird Floyd will carve and paint in this book is a mature female eastern hawk, light phase. You can tailor the color phase to suit you by consulting reference material such as photographs, live birds, or mounted specimens.

Indeed, before beginning any bird-carving project, it is important to learn all you can about your subject—not only what the bird looks like, but how it acts. Photographs and mounted birds are invaluable for researching fine detail, such as how the dark spots that make up the belly band are organized. But it is also important to spend time in the field, observing and listening and simply experiencing a bird as it goes about its daily business. For many artists, this is the most important part of the research; there is often some decisive moment when a bird catches the light just right, or gracefully preens itself, and the artist realizes that this is the way he wants to depict the bird in wood.

FLOYD SCHOLZ

A beautiful head portrait of an adult red-tailed hawk shows the bill and cere detail. Pay careful attention to the size and shape of the eyelid and to the feather flow around the eyes.

Note the exposed primary feathers and primary covert feathers on this adult red-tailed hawk. These indicate motion, as if the hawk might open a wing or shift his weight on the perch.

TAD MERRICK

8

This bird assumes a defensive posture, spreading his wings and raising his crest feathers to look much larger than he really is.

Here you see the angle and shape of the foot, leg, and tarsus feathers, and how they join the body. The tarsus feathers have an almost fur-like softness.

CHAPTER THREE

Getting Started

The red-tailed hawk is a large bird, and the project will require a large piece of wood. Floyd uses tupelo gum, which he purchases from Curt's Waterfowl Corner in Montegut, Louisiana. The wood is stored in a barn, and Floyd ages it for at least four years before carving. This gives it a chance to stabilize and adjust to the Vermont climate.

Floyd will cut a blank from a large piece of tupelo for carving the hawk. The blank will be 2 inches longer than the actual dimensions of the bird to allow for squaring and to avoid any splits that might occur along the end grain. The block will be roughly $8^1/_4$ inches wide by 6 inches deep by 21 inches long.

"You develop a feel for tupelo over the years," says Floyd. "You can tap it and lift it, and based on its weight and feel, you can tell if it's going to be a good piece. I like to use a pocketknife to slice off a piece and look closely at the grain. If it's dark and very grainy or if it feels especially heavy, I tend to avoid it."

Floyd uses a 1963 model 20-inch Powermatic band saw to cut the blank from the large piece of tupelo and to do the preliminary roughing out of the bird. If you don't have a band saw, you can have a woodworking shop do the work for you. If you do use power tools, be sure to read and understand the safety instructions that came with them. Also, it's important to wear safety glasses when using power tools and to use ear protectors when operating noisy equipment. Some type of air filter or exhaustion system is necessary to remove fine dust, which can damage the lungs.

Once the block is cut to size, Floyd runs it through a jointer to make sure the sides are perfectly flat and at right angles. He then draws a centerline, which in this case will be at $4^1/_8$ inches. "The centerline is all-important, even at this preliminary stage, and I will refer to it often almost until painting," says Floyd.

Using a cardboard pattern, Floyd sketches the side profile of the bird, then cuts it out, leaving plenty of wood in the area of the head so he can make adjustments in the angle or tilt of the head later. "I like to leave that extra wood to give myself more latitude," he says. "The personality of the bird is in the head. You can tell a lot about the attitude of a bird by the position and balance of the head and neck area."

When the side profile is cut, Floyd redraws the centerline, and then lays out the front-back pattern. He band saws it out, again leaving plenty of wood for the head.

Once the block is roughed out, Floyd uses the band saw to round off edges and remove any excess wood he can safely reach. Floyd is experienced in using the band saw. If you are not, it would be safer to do the final stages of roughing out with a high-speed grinder or a wood rasp.

Floyd begins by sorting through his collection of tupelo wood. He uses wood that has seasoned for at least four years.

The hawk is a large bird and will require a block of wood 8¼ by 6 by 21 inches. Floyd allows 2 extra inches in length to eliminate any end-grain splits.

Floyd carefully inspects the wood, making sure it is not too dense and grainy. He uses a pocketknife to slice off a piece and inspects the grain.

The block that will be used for the hawk is cut from a larger piece of tupelo. If you are not familiar with using a band saw, you can have a woodshop do this for you.

Floyd uses the jointer to true up two edges, ensuring that he has a flat surface and a perfect right angle. He then draws a centerline, measuring the width of the block. This particular one is 8$1/4$ inches wide at the shoulders, so the centerline is at 4$1/8$ inches.

Floyd checks the dimensions of the block against the front pattern. The thickness and width are perfect.

Floyd draws the side profile of the bird first, using a cardboard pattern. He will cut this out and then trace on the back pattern.

Floyd cuts the side profile on the band saw, leaving plenty of wood in the area of the head so that he can later make adjustments in the angle or tilt.

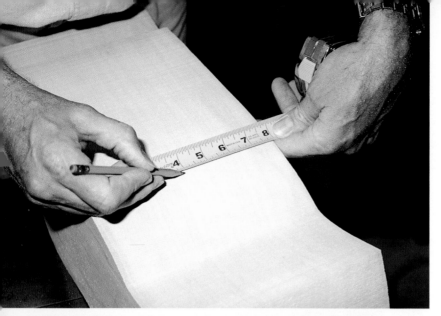

When the side profile is cut, Floyd redraws the center-line, which is now at $3\frac{7}{8}$ inches. The centerline will be maintained throughout the carving process.

Floyd now lays out and sketches the front pattern, then roughs it out on the band saw.

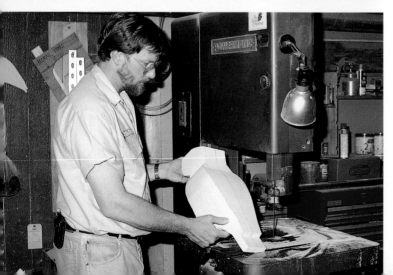

After the front and side profiles are cut, the carving looks like this. Note that the centerline runs along the body and over the head.

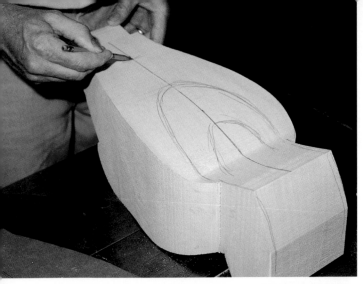

Floyd frequently sketches on the wood as part of the planning process. Here he sketches in the primary feather groups—the nape area, scapulars, secondaries, tertials, and primaries.

Floyd uses a carpenter's square to determine the angle at which the head is turned and to redraw the centerline at that angle.

The head will be turned slightly to the left, and Floyd draws in this angle, beginning where the center-line on the back intersects with the head.

15

Floyd uses the band saw to round off edges and remove any excess wood he can safely reach. "The band saw is a very useful tool, a real time-saver, but it can also be dangerous," says Floyd. "You can easily cut away too much wood and turn the red-tailed hawk into a kestrel, or you can cut yourself badly. If you're not experienced with the tool, have a professional cut the block out for you."

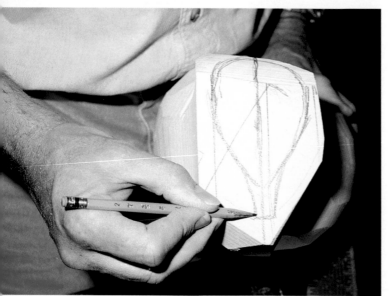

With the centerline of the head established, Floyd uses top and side profile patterns to lay out the head and neck area. The top profile is sketched in the direction of the centerline—that is, angled slightly to the left.

The band saw is used to remove excess wood in the head area. You could use a high-speed grinder instead.

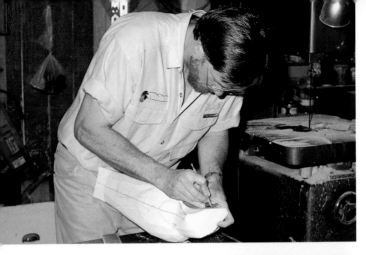

With the top profile roughed out, Floyd sketches the side profile and cuts that to size.

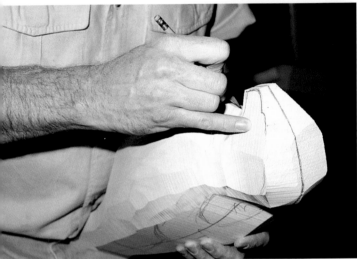

The hawk is now roughed out and is ready for more detailed carving, which will be done with a Foredom high-speed grinder. Note that Floyd left a little extra wood in the bill area on this carving.

At this stage, the maximum blocked dimensions are close to those of the finished bird; the width of the shoulders in this roughed-out version is roughly what it will be when the bird is finished, slightly less than 8 inches.

CHAPTER FOUR

Roughing Out the Major Feather Groups

With the block roughed out on the band saw, Floyd is now ready to add the major feather groups. He begins with the upper part of the bird, at the nape, and progresses downward along the scapulars, tertials, primaries, and tail.

It's important at this stage to have good reference material and to know the correct shape and size of these feather groups. The patterns included in this book are intended to make the carving process easier for you, but it is still important to study the real bird and to get a feel for avian anatomy—to understand not only the various feather groups of the wing, but also how they work.

The carving process is fairly straightforward. Floyd sketches the positions of the feather groups with a soft lead pencil, then he uses the sanding drum to cut along the pencil line, leaving a sharp ledge that later will be rounded off. The depth of the ledge varies according to the size of the feather group. The nape, a relatively small area, is defined by a ledge about 1/8 inch; the wings, however, are undercut by about 1/2 inch.

The same tool is used throughout this chapter. It is a Foredom flexible shaft grinder equipped with a 1-by-2-inch rubber sanding drum mounted on a 1/4-inch shaft. The tool allows Floyd to remove a great deal of wood quickly and to do so in long, sweeping strokes that help maintain symmetry and flowing lines. Floyd uses 50-grit sandpaper on the drum and keeps a large supply of it on hand.

It's important to maintain the centerline during this roughing-out phase. It is essential for maintaining the proper dimensions of the bird, and Floyd measures from the centerline when laying out feather groups. If part of the line is obliterated during the rounding-out process, immediately redraw it.

In this chapter, Floyd will shape the back of the bird, defining the wings, tail, and nape, and he will round off the chest and neck area. When he has finished, the back will be ready for individual feathers.

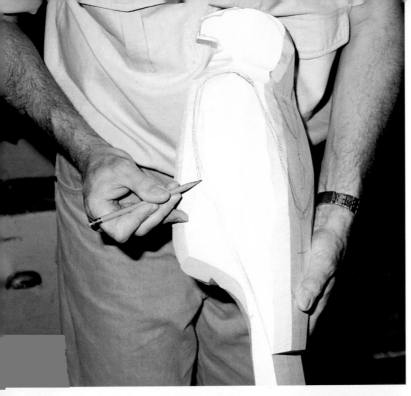

With the block roughed out on the band saw, Floyd takes it into his studio for subsequent shaping. He uses a pencil to sketch the major feather groups, working from big to small.

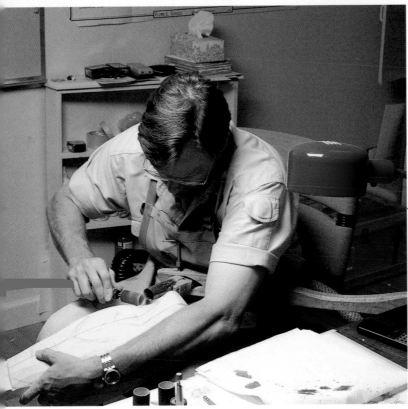

He begins with the shoulders and upper back, working from the centerline. Sanding creates a lot of airborne dust, and Floyd removes it by using a vacuum cleaner with the nozzle positioned a few inches from the tool.

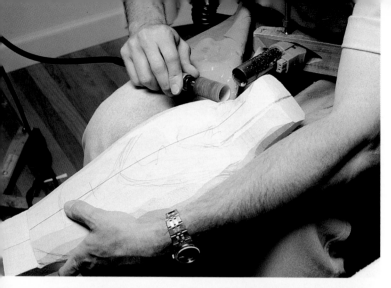

For rough shaping, Floyd's favorite tool is a Foredom flexible shaft grinder fitted with a 1-by-2-inch rubber sanding drum. He uses 50-grit paper.

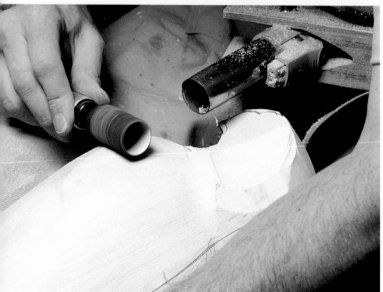

Floyd works on the left side of the bird first, then moves to the right side. "I get the left side rounded down to about halfway, then I switch to the other side," he says. "Whatever you do to one side, immediately repeat it on the other. You can't completely carve one side of the bird and then the other; you have do it in stages, step by step."

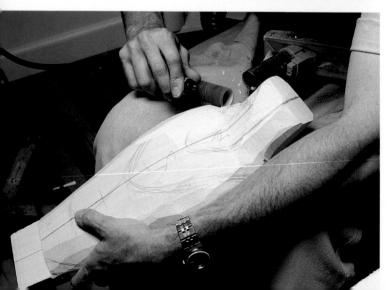

At this early stage, Floyd is simply rounding off contours and will relieve the major feather groupings he earlier sketched with the pencil.

"What you're striving for in the roughing-out stage is symmetry," he says. "No matter how well you carve and paint, if the bird is not symmetrical, it will look off-balance and it won't look real. Stay with your centerline, be very careful with your measurements, and always try to achieve balance and symmetry."

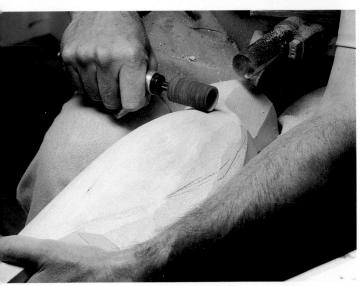

Floyd now has the back of the bird rounded off, and next he will add the feather groups, cutting a shallow line along the margins of these groups to create what will become a layered look.

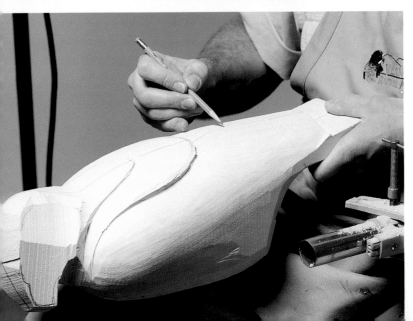

Floyd lays out the major feather groups on the back of the bird, beginning at the shoulder with the nape and extending downward to the top of the tertials.

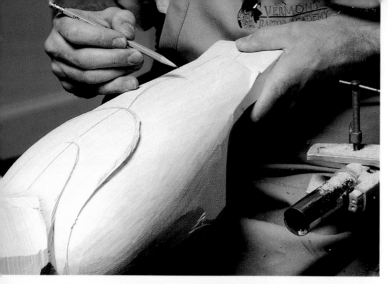

If the centerline has been obliterated during the rounding-out process, redraw it now. It's essential to work from the centerline when measuring and laying out these large feather groups.

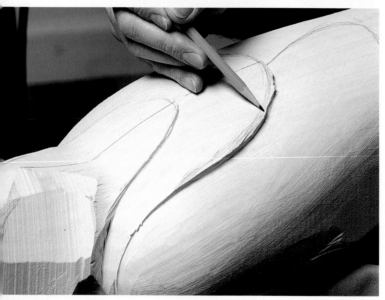

The shallow shelf that defines each group is about 1/4 inch deep. It will be rounded off later.

The scapulars are 5 1/8 inches wide, so Floyd measures off the centerline on each side 2 9/16 to determine the margins of this group.

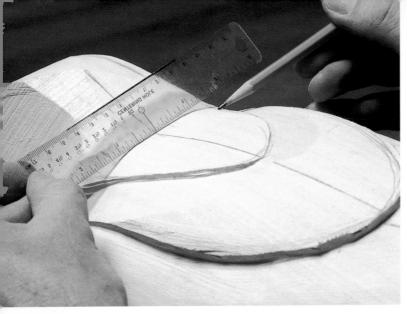

Above the scapulars is the nape, which is 3 inches wide, so Floyd measures 1 1/2 inches off the centerline and relieves this area, leaving a shelf about 1/8 inch deep.

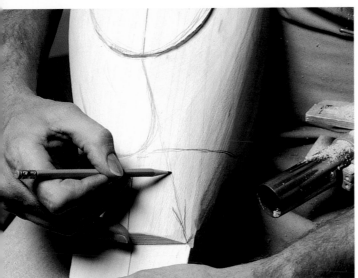

Floyd now pencils in the tertial feathers. The tertials are the large, platelike feathers that lie on the uppermost end of the secondary feather track. At this point, it's important to determine which wing will overlap the other. With this bird, the head is turned to the left, so Floyd makes the left wing dominant, on top of the right wing.

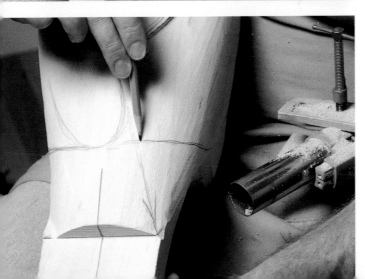

Floyd pencils in the outer dimensions of the tertials, starting where the centerline joins the lowest point of the scapular group. He draws a straight line from that point to the band saw mark where the primary notch joins the top of the tail surface.

23

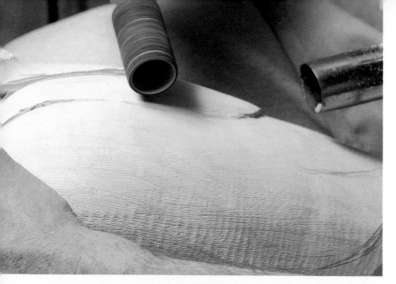

The sanding drum is used to round off the edges of the feather groups, making them more subtle.

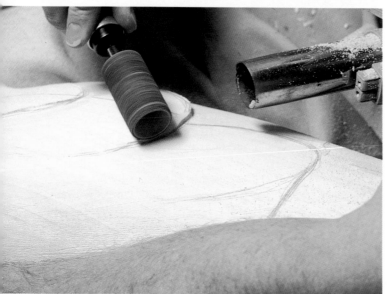

The edges of the feather groups should appear to be slightly rounded and overlapping. Work to avoid a shelf—or step—where one group overlaps another. Subtlety is important in these areas.

Once these two top feather groups have been rounded, Floyd redraws the centerline in preparation for laying out the larger wing feather groups.

The pencil is used to sketch the locations of the primary and secondary feathers, which are carved using the same technique as on the nape and scapulars. On these large feather groups, Floyd uses long, sweeping strokes with the sanding drum.

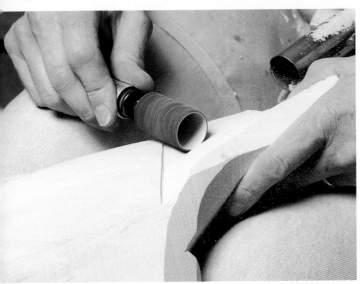

Floyd draws in the rough shape and carves around the perimeter. "It's a sequential process going from the top of the back to the tail. We begin at the nape and then go to the scapulars, tertials, primaries, and the tail, which is given a slightly rounded shape."

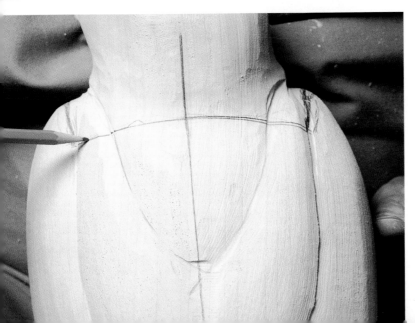

Floyd draws a line across the nape perpendicular to the centerline and continues it to the outer edge of the scapulars. That will be the starting point for carving the wing separation, defining the leading edge of each wing.

Working from where the line intersects the wing, Floyd draws an arching line that defines the margins of the wings. Again, strive for consistency and symmetry when drawing these lines; don't make one higher or larger than the other.

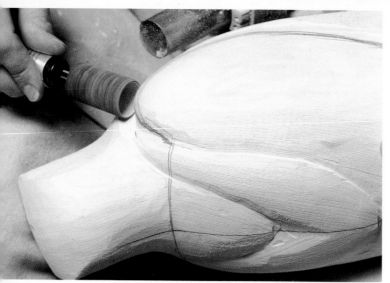

Floyd uses the sanding cylinder to cut along this line, leaving a ledge of about 1/2 inch. This line separates the wings from the chest area.

This step goes quickly, Floyd says, but completely changes the shape of the bird. With the wings defined, the block of wood is slowly beginning to look more birdlike.

Wood is removed at a 90-degree angle to the surface using the same technique as on the other feather groups, but the shelf is more severe, approximately 1/2 inch.

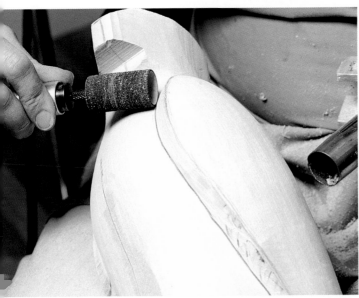

The left wing is taking shape. The hard edge will be rounded off with the sanding tool, as before. Careful study of a live bird will reveal a strongly curved wing surface, especially toward the leading edge of the wing.

Both the right and left wings are now near completion. Floyd rounds off the ledge, defining the wings, and he also rounds out the chest, neck, belly, and flank sections.

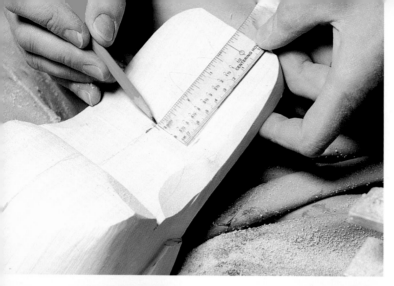

Floyd now lays out the undertail covert feathers, those large, fluffy feathers that cover the bottom of the tail. He measures 3½ inches from the tip of the tail to the coverts and makes a mark.

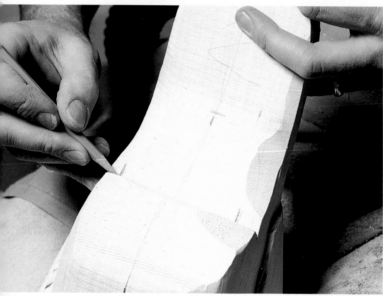

He then measures out 1¾ inches from the centerline on each side to create a triangle.

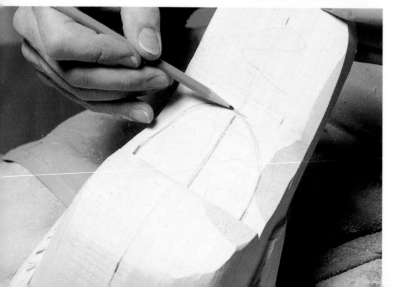

"From there it's a matter of connecting the dots," says Floyd. This arched line defines the undertail coverts.

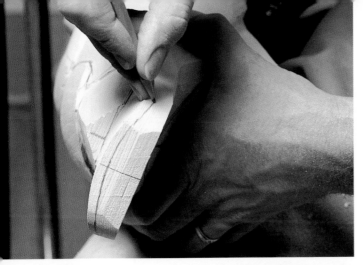

The tail must now be reduced to its proper thickness and carved with a downward taper on each side. Floyd holds a pencil and, using his middle finger as a gauge, draws a line from the top roughly 1/4 inch thick. This line represents roughly the thickness of the tail, and Floyd will use it as a guide when removing wood. The line follows the slight curve earlier given to the top of the tail feathers.

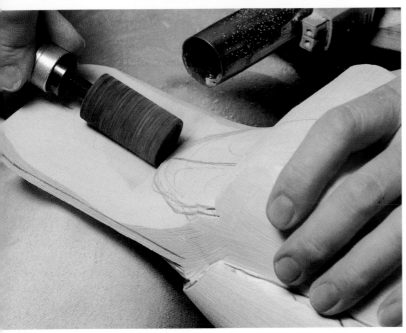

At this point, Floyd uses the sanding drum to remove waste wood. "Most carvers fail to go deep enough in this area, which results in a thick, blocky tail," he says.

This process reduces the tail feathers to the proper thickness and also defines the undertail covert group.

The tail is now reduced to near proper thickness. The edges will later be thinned further, but the tail itself needs to be fairly thick to retain strength.

The next step is to rough in the legs. Floyd does this by first measuring $3/4$ inch off the centerline and drawing two parallel lines that will represent the inner sides of the legs.

He uses the sanding drum to plow a channel $1^1/_2$ inches wide from the chest back to the undertail covert feathers. This step establishes the rough location of the legs.

CHAPTER FIVE

Carving the Head

The head was roughed out on the band saw, and now Floyd is ready to do some detail carving. In this chapter, he will round off the head, reduce it to proper dimensions, shape the bill, carve the eye groove, and insert the glass eye. These steps will really breathe some life into the red-tail.

Floyd sketches the top dimensions of the head by measuring from the centerline. For the side profile, he uses the pattern reproduced in this book. The sanding drum is used for the rough shaping, and smaller cutters for the fine work.

Cutting the eye groove is an important step in carving the head. Floyd cuts the groove deeply, giving the bird a prominent brow. "Louis Agassiz Fuertes always painted raptors with a furrowed brow, kind of a scowl. That's the look I want here," Floyd says.

Floyd will carve the two channels and round off the head, careful to avoid a boxy shape. He uses a 1/2-inch ruby stone, cutting in the same direction the feathers will flow.

Care must also be taken when carving the bill. "A common mistake beginners make is not to go deep enough on the jaw and lip regions of the bird," says Floyd. "This area needs to be pinched in quite a bit, or it will look like a frog's mouth."

A key word in this chapter, as it has been throughout, is *symmetry*. Details such as the eyes, nostrils, brow ridge, and cere must be balanced and symmetrical. One eye must not be higher or lower than the other, nor one brow ridge more prominent. To ensure balance and symmetry, Floyd carefully measures where he can and always sketches detail before carving it.

Until now, Floyd has used only the sanding drum mounted on a Foredom flexible-shaft tool. In this chapter, he will use a variety of smaller, finer cutting tools with a high-speed grinder, as well as a pyrographic instrument, or burning pen, for fine detail in the bill. Cutting tools come in a great variety of shapes and sizes, and selection is to a large extent a personal choice. If you feel more comfortable using a tip you are familiar with, then by all means do so.

Floyd uses the centerline as a reference when sketching the shape of the top of the head and bill. This ensures symmetry—the head will not be wider on one side than the other. The heavy line perpendicular to the centerline represents the separation between head and bill.

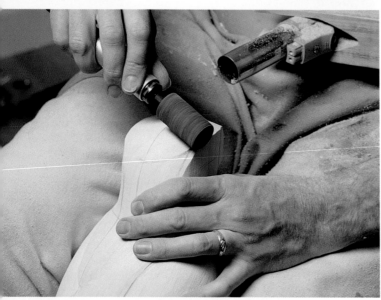

Floyd uses the sanding drum to round off the sides of the head, using the sketch made in the previous step as a guide.

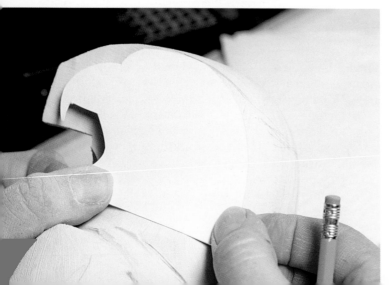

A paper pattern of the side profile, reproduced in this book, is placed on the side of the head, and a pencil is used to sketch the outline.

Floyd left plenty of excess wood when he roughed out the carving, so he has some leeway when positioning the side profile.

The sanding drum is used to do the rough carving of the bill and head. "Be sure to proceed slowly in this delicate area," Floyd says, "and check your work frequently against your reference material."

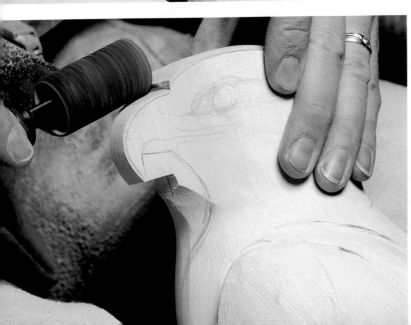

Floyd cuts a notch on top of the bill, separating it from the head. He is careful to follow the lines established by the pattern.

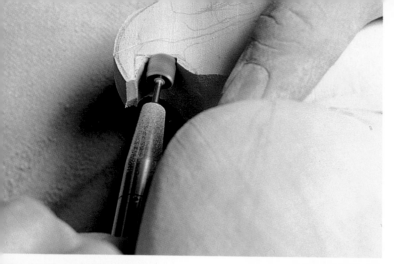

For tight spots, Floyd switches to smaller tools. This stump cutter is perfect for shaping the area under the bill.

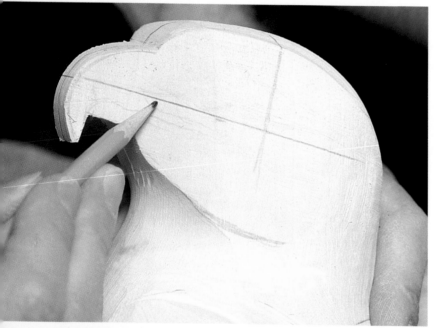

With the head and bill reduced to near final dimensions, Floyd is ready to carve the eye groove of the hawk. He first draws a horizontal line representing the jaw line, and then he draws a second line above it that defines the top brow ridge.

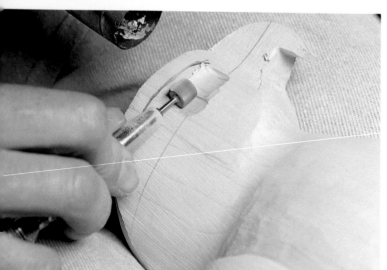

Floyd makes a deep plow cut on each side of the head, following the two pencil lines. He uses a stump cutter for preliminary carving and then will switch to a 1/2-inch round stone, which gives a smoother cut.

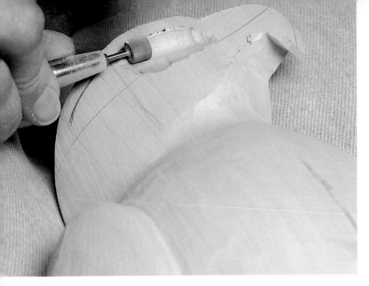

The plow cuts are widest at the eye areas and are tapered down to the width of the beak where the beak joins the head.

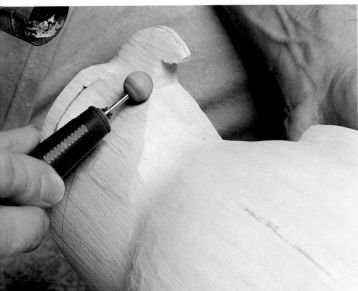

The 1/2-inch round ruby cutter is used to round off the edges of the plow cut and make it more subtle, a technique very similar to the one Floyd used when carving the feather groupings.

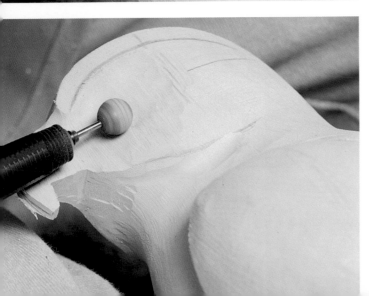

The ball is used to reduce and shape the face immediately behind the bill. "Don't hesitate to really deepen the eye channel as it resolves into the cere and bill areas," says Floyd.

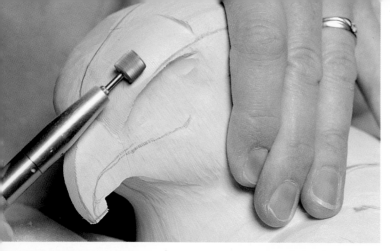

Floyd goes back to the stump cutter to round off the brow and blend it into the top of the head.

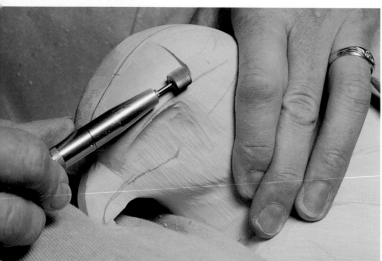

It's important at this step not to take off too much wood. Floyd wants the brow rounded, but he also wants to keep it prominent. A lot of the bird's personality is captured in this area.

Here again, symmetry is important. As you carve the eye grooves and brow, check frequently to make sure they are balanced.

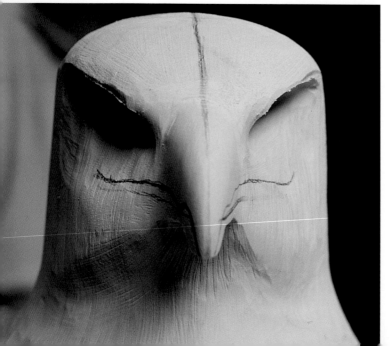

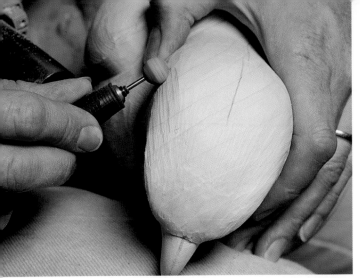

The cutting tools, such as this round ball, are used in the direction of the feather flow. This provides a little preliminary texturing, a foundation for the finer detail that will come later.

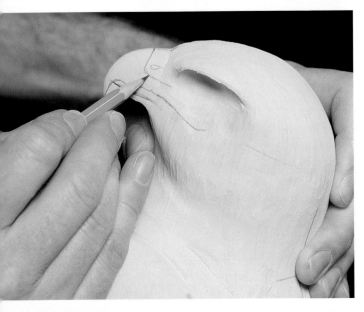

Floyd uses the pencil to sketch bill detail before carving. Here he has penciled in the nostrils, cere, lip, and the separation between the upper and lower mandibles.

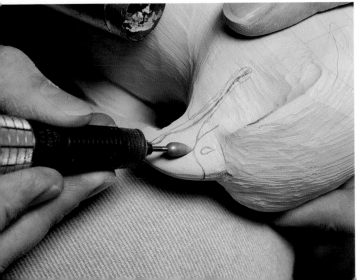

A flame-tip ruby cutter is used to carve along the lines that separate the cere from the bill. The bill is reduced slightly here, making the cere prominent.

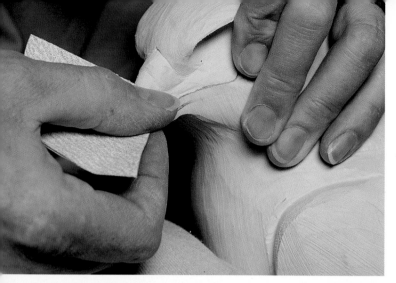

Floyd uses the burning pen to carve the separation between the mandibles, but first he smooths the area with fine sandpaper.

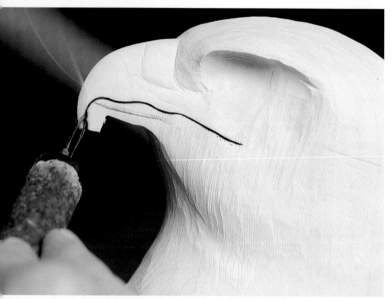

Floyd burns along the lip and on the line between the upper and lower beak. The burning pen is set on medium-high temperature.

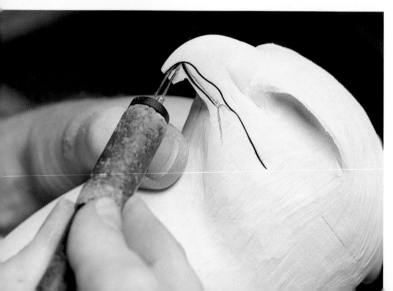

He burns deeply so that after subsequent sandings the line will still show. Floyd feels that burning is preferable to cutting because it doesn't tear the wood. Also, a knife blade could split the wood in this fragile area.

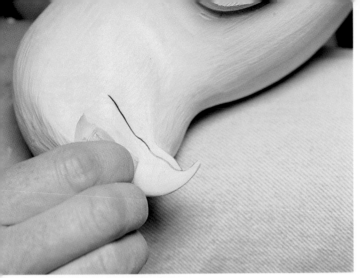

Floyd now is ready to add the nostrils, but first he lightly sands the area of the cere, the fleshy upper part of the bill where the nostrils are located.

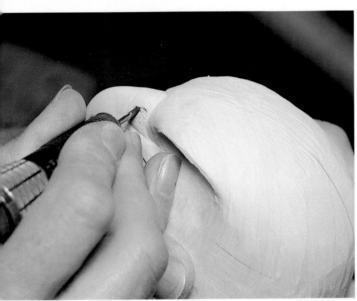

A pointed diamond tip is used to cut out the nostril area. Because absolute accuracy is essential, Floyd rests his hand against the head so that he can steady the cutter.

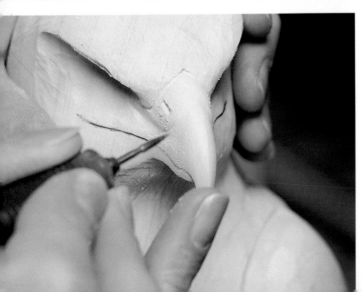

It's very important that the nostrils be in alignment; sketch them in pencil before carving, and look at the bird from the front to make sure they are the same size and symmetrical.

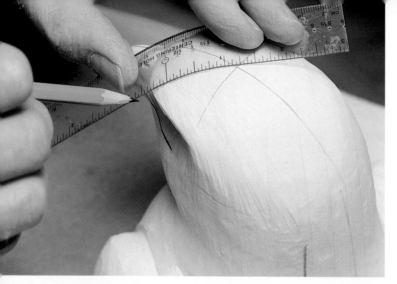

The eyes of buteos usually fall at about a 45-degree angle to the centerline of the head. Floyd lays this out in a grid, again using the centerline as a reference.

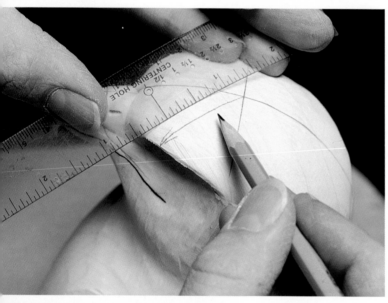

He first draws a line perpendicular to the centerline, then draws a second line at a 45-degree angle. He will drill the eye socket in the direction of this line.

Floyd uses dividers to make sure the eyes are the same distance from the tip of the bill. Here he has sketched in the left eye and is measuring the distance from the center of the eye to the tip of the bill.

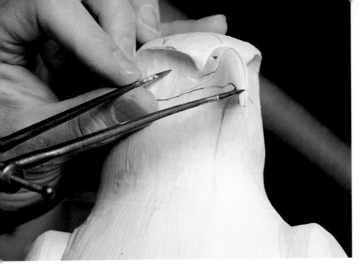

That measurement is then transferred to the right side of the head. "There is no mathematical way to determine the eye location exactly," says Floyd. "You need to use your own eye to determine what looks good and what doesn't. Spend lots of time studying birds and learn them well."

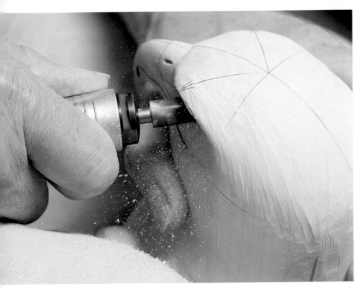

A 1/2-inch spur bit designed specifically for eye insertion is used to drill the eye hole. The bit is held at the indicated 45-degree angle as the hole is drilled.

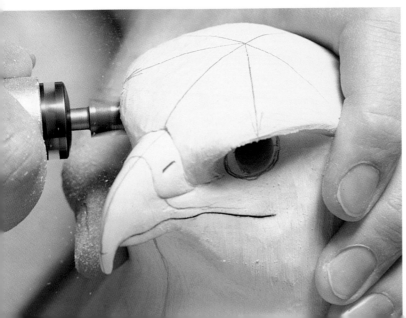

The left eye is drilled first, then the right. Floyd rechecks the eye position with dividers before drilling, making sure the eyes are in alignment.

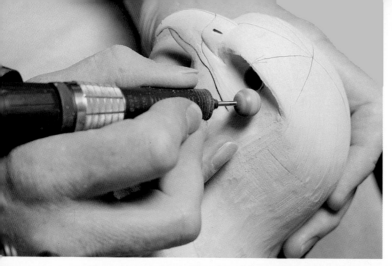

Floyd drills the initial hole slightly smaller than the diameter of the glass eye. He uses a stone tip to enlarge the hole, undercutting the brow. This enables him to mount the eye under the brow without having to cut through it.

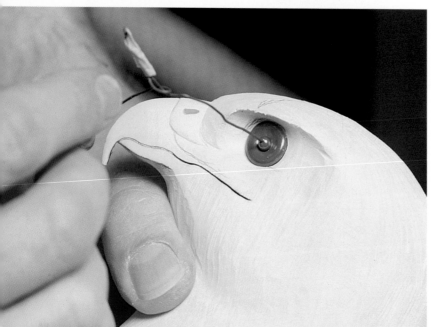

The eye is trial-fitted until it is just snug. A too-tight fit will not allow adjustments once the eyes are set. "It's okay to have a small amount of the putty ooze out around the eye," Floyd says. "You can blend the excess putty into the surrounding wood to form a good seal."

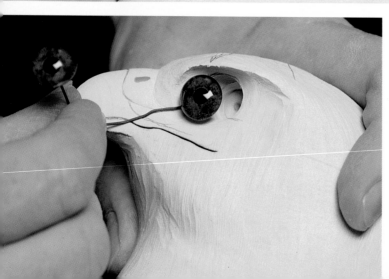

Floyd will leave about 1/8-inch of wire on the glass eye to ensure proper seating and alignment. Two-part epoxy medium is applied to the hole before the eye is pressed in. Later, the eye will be finished by application of an epoxy membrane.

CHAPTER SIX

Adding Individual Feathers

The feather groups have been defined, and now it's time to carve some individual feathers. Later, we'll take the process even farther and use the burning pen to add barbs and quills. But for now, Floyd is going to carve individual feathers, specifically the large flight feathers of the wings and tail.

Using a mounted bird as reference, Floyd first draws the feather with a pencil, then carves it with either the sanding drum mounted in the Foredom or a small stone bit in his Gesswein high-speed grinder.

Floyd advises carvers to take some license when drawing and carving these tail and flight feathers. Every feather does not have to show, and you should avoid making them appear too uniform. "The red-tail has twelve tail feathers, but sometimes the bird loses one or two, or it may be going through a molt," he says. "When the tail is tucked very tightly, not all the feathers will show, so don't worry about carving the exact number."

Floyd draws the feathers, varying the spacing between them. "Don't be too uniform. You don't want them looking like little window blinds," he advises.

Now Floyd carves each feather, using much the same technique as for the feather groups. Then he softens the edges with a sanding mandrel, making the effect more subtle. "The effect you want is that of a bunch of grapes," says Floyd. "All the feathers should blend together somewhat. They shouldn't be uniform, all in a line, with no ledges or steps. The distinction between them should be subtle. The mandrel is good for doing that, and you also can use it to carve little bumps and ripples. The idea is to make the bird as lifelike as possible. That's why you need to study live birds, photographs, mounts, and any other good reference material you can find."

Floyd will begin with the tail feathers and work his way up the back of the bird.

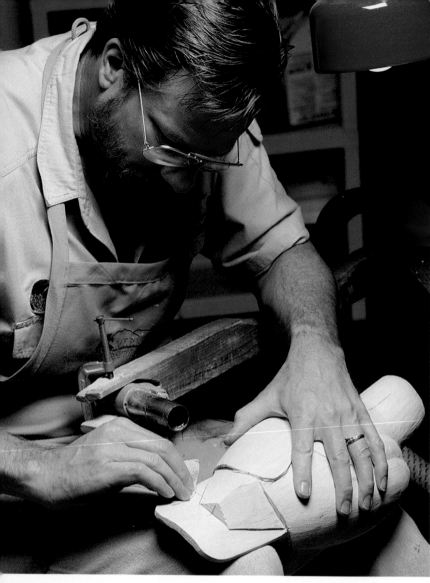

Floyd uses 100-grit aluminum oxide sandpaper to smooth the wood surface where he will draw in the feather groups.

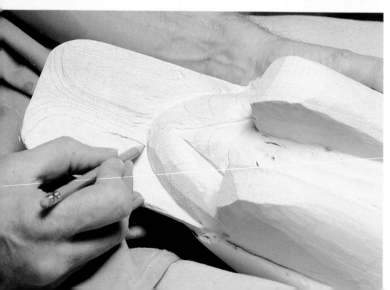

He begins with the underside of the tail, drawing in the individual feathers. The hawk has twelve tail feathers, but it's not imperative to show each one.

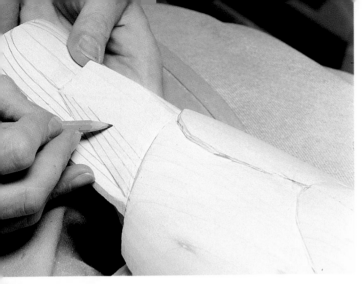

The tail feathers are sketched on the top of the bird, as are the primary feathers of the wings. Floyd advises not to make the feathers too regimented and uniform.

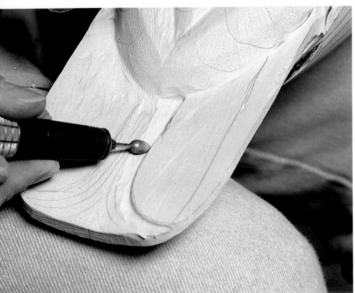

Initial carving is done with a Gesswein high-speed grinder with a tapered ruby tip. A Gesswein slender head is extremely useful for this application.

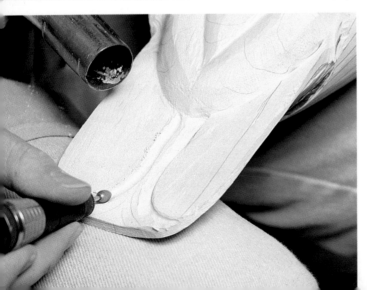

Floyd cuts a groove along each pencil line, thus defining the feathers. A flame-shaped ruby carver is very useful in shaping this concave area under the tail.

He uses sandpaper under the tail to smooth the edges cut with the Gesswein.

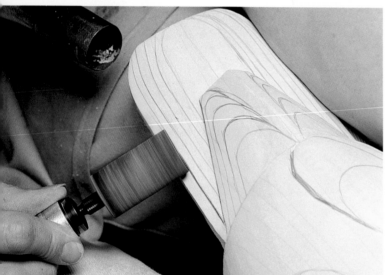

On the top of the tail, Floyd carves the tail feathers with the sanding drum. He varies the depth of the individual feathers, undercutting some to give the appearance of fullness.

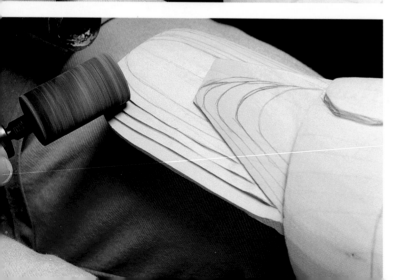

He cuts along each pencil line, creating a layered appearance. Floyd then sands and gently curves the edges of the feathers so that they appear more natural.

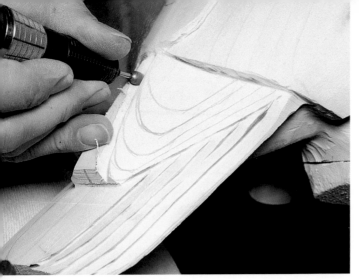

The primary feathers are carved with the tapered tip of the Gesswein. These feathers get thinner and pointier toward the tail, so the longest primary will be the slimmest. As they approach the tertials and secondaries, the primary feathers get broader and more rounded, eventually matching the shape of the secondaries.

The feather shafts gradually migrate toward the center of the feather as they get the higher on the bird.

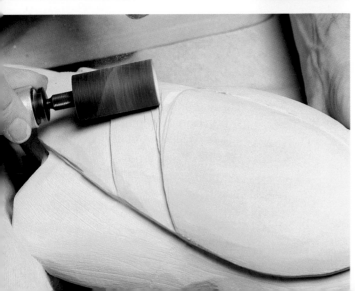

The sanding drum is used to relieve the feather groups of the wings. At this stage, Floyd is defining the groups rather than the individual feathers. It's essential to know the different feather groups, their shapes, and their functions.

As in previous steps, Floyd first pencils in the feather groups, and then defines them by cutting a line along each pencil mark. He works his way up the back of the hawk.

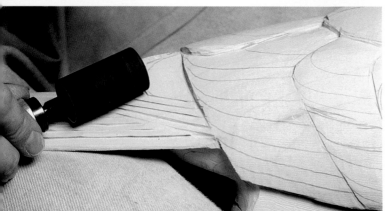

Before he finishes with the sanding drum, he uses it to gently sand the primary and tail feathers, making the edges more subtle.

The tapered ruby cutter is used to add a few grooves to the primaries. Floyd notes, "You can vary the size and depth of these grooves, but don't overdo it."

These grooves will later become subtle ripples or folds, which will add to the lifelike quality of the carving.

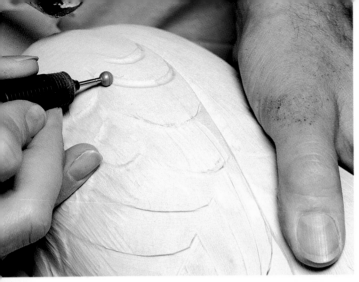

A 1/4-inch ruby ball is used in the grinder to define the upper median covert feathers on the right wing, which are first sketched with a pencil. This ball is used to carve the larger feathers; Floyd changes to smaller stones for smaller feathers.

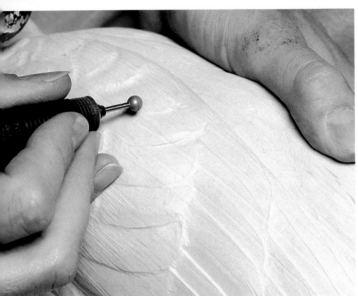

The procedure for carving these feathers is similar to that used previously. Floyd sketches the feathers with a pencil, cuts along the pencil line with the ruby ball, and later will smooth the carved line with sandpaper loaded in a split mandrel.

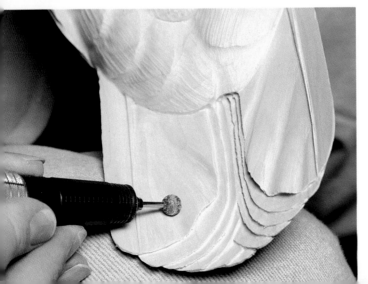

It's important to add some lifelike splits, curves, and subtle ripples to feathers. Floyd does this with the ruby ball, applied here to one of the tail feathers.

Sandpaper is used to smooth the margins of the furrow cut with the ball.

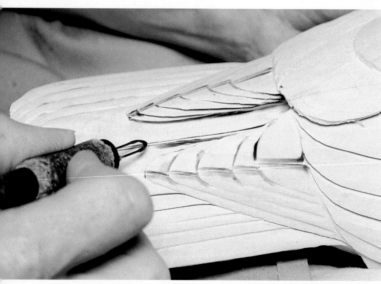

The shafts and feather edges on the upper tail are defined with the burning pen. To create a shaft, Floyd cuts two parallel lines with the woodburner on medium heat, tapering the lines to a point at the tip of the feather.

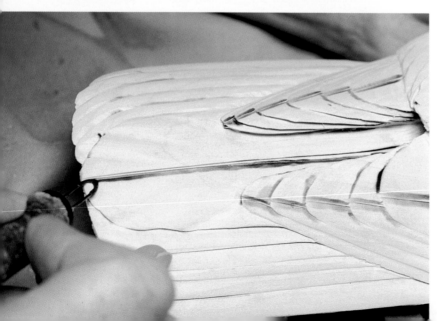

On the upper tail feathers, where the shaft is not that prominent, Floyd uses the side of the burning tip, pressing it slightly against the wood to compress the fibers. This creates a subtle ridge that represents the shaft.

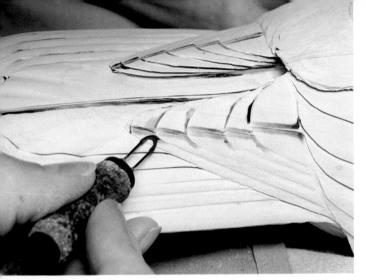

Here the technique is used to create a shaft on one of the primary feathers.

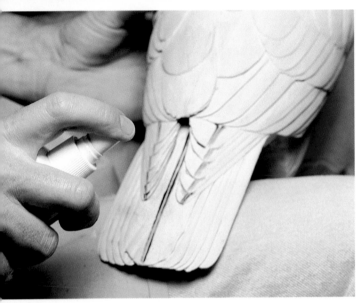

Floyd applies a mist of rubbing alcohol to raise the grain before sanding the feathers.

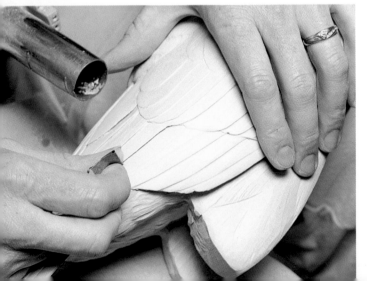

The feathers are finally sanded with 600-grit paper to remove all scratch lines that might have been left by the cutting tools.

This photo also shows the still-rough tarsus areas. When these areas have been fully carved and textured, Floyd will use a 1/4-inch wood drill to create 2-inch sockets for the leg shafts. Placement of the sockets will depend on the alignment of bird and base.

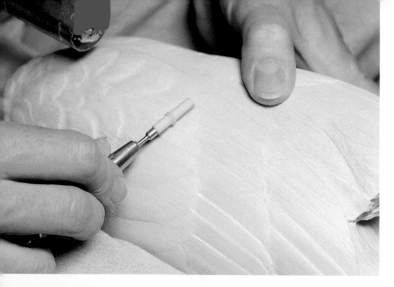

A split mandrel is used with 150-grit sandpaper to smooth the edges of the individual feathers carved earlier.

"Avoid having sharp ledges and steps," says Floyd. "These feathers are very soft, and the edges should be subtle."

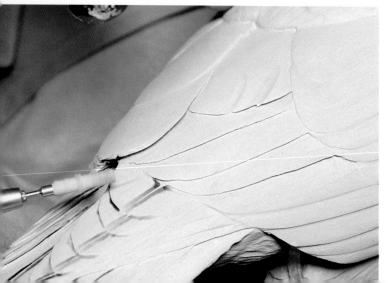

The sandpaper is held in the mandrel by a small rubber band of the type used in orthodontics. The grinder is used at about one-third speed when sanding.

Floyd also uses the mandrel to create little ripples and curves in individual feathers. It leaves texture lines very similar to those of real feathers.

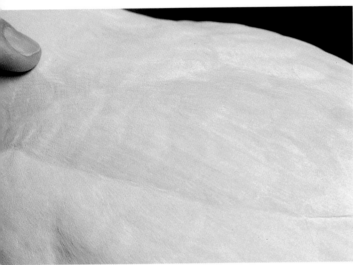

With the edges sanded, the individual feathers carved on the back are now very subtle, and are beginning to take on the illusion of softness.

The mandrel is also used to do some preliminary sanding around the head. "Some carvers wait to set the eyes until *after* the head has been fully sanded and textured," Floyd says. "It's a matter of personal preference—whatever works best for you."

CHAPTER SEVEN

Burning and Texturing

The final step in the carving process is to add texture to the individual feathers. This means, for the most part, using the burning pen to carefully scribe small lines representing the texture of feathers. It also means using a stone tool with the grinder to add little bumps and lines that will make the wooden surface appear soft and downy. A stone cylinder is used to add feather barbs on small, soft-edged feathers. These techniques, coupled with subsequent soft washes of paint, will produce a surface that looks remarkably realistic.

But before Floyd begins the burning and texturing process, he will carefully hand-sand all surfaces of wood, actually polishing it to as smooth a surface as possible. Sanding will remove any scratches or marks left by the carving tools, and it will produce the extremely smooth surface that is necessary for fine burning.

"Sanding is boring, hard work and absolutely no fun, but the end result is without question worth the effort," says Floyd. "It gives you an ideal surface for burning, and that, in turn, will produce a fine, soft paint job. The finer the burn, the better the paint. Sanding is time well spent. Take it down to 600-grit and use alcohol mist. That produces the polished surface."

Floyd begins sanding with 120-grit paper, progresses to 150-, 320-, and finally 600-grit, which is preceded by a light spray of rubbing alcohol, raising the grain and helping to produce a smooth, glasslike surface.

When that is done, he uses a small burnishing ball on the Gesswein to add a few bumps and ripples that help create the illusion of softness. A pencil is used to sketch in the individual feathers, and then Floyd begins the process of burning in the feather texture. The burning pen is used for this because it compresses rather than removes the wood and thus can create very fine detail. Floyd will etch about one hundred lines per inch with the burning pen.

Basically, Floyd uses two different burning tips and two different techniques. A spear-shaped tip is used to carve the feather shafts and other details such as feather splits, and a skew tip is used for burning the fine barbs.

When burning barbs on large feathers, Floyd works from the shaft outward. With the small feathers of the upper back and head, he burns from the outside of the feather, pulling the tool toward the shaft.

Most of the feathers on the hawk are textured with the burning pen, but some are textured with a cylinder mounted in the Gesswein grinder. Generally, Floyd burns feathers that are large and have visible edges and feathers that are dark. He uses the stone cylinder on small, loose feathers that have ragged edges. Those on the breast and belly of the hawk will be stoned, for example, while the large flight feathers and those of the back and head will be burned.

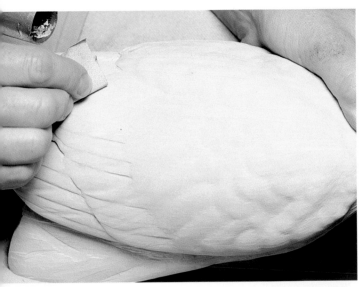

To get clean burn lines, the wood surface should be carefully sanded. Floyd begins with 120-grit paper, progresses to 150-, 320-, and finally 600-grit, which is preceded by a light misting of rubbing alcohol, raising the grain and helping to produce a smooth, glasslike surface.

With the surface sanded and polished, Floyd begins drawing the individual feathers, establishing the flow and pattern. "I use a technique I call 'feather acceleration,'" he says. "I decrease the size of the feather as it nears its point of origin and increase it toward the tip."

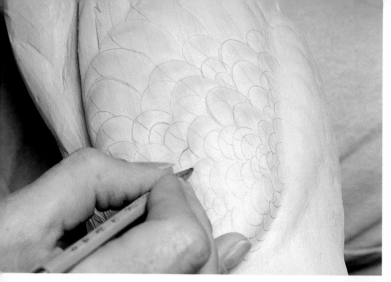

Floyd also varies the size of the feathers. "You want to avoid a fish-scale look," he says. "Alter the size, gradually decreasing it as you approach the point of origin of the feather. Though it may sound contradictory, you want the feathers to look random but organized." Once the feathers are drawn, Floyd adds the shafts, again placing them in a random manner.

The shafts are carved with a spear-point tip on the burning pen. The shafts should be staggered so that the shaft of one feather doesn't fall in line with the one next to it.

Floyd burns two nearly parallel lines on either side of the penciled shaft, converging the lines as the shaft comes to a point at the end of the feather. This depresses the wood around the shaft and leaves a slight ridge, which represents the shaft. The shafts should be carved with a slight arc to accentuate the roundness of the feather. This helps create a three-dimensional look.

With the feather shafts burned, Floyd uses a burnishing ball in his Gesswein grinder to create small creases in the feathers that will add to the illusion of softness.

The shafts have been burned on the wings and texturing has been added with the burnishing ball, which is a round ruby cutter with most of the abrasive removed. The hawk is now ready for individual feather barbs.

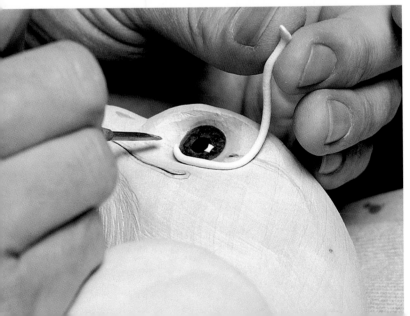

Before burning the feather barbs and texturing the head, Floyd adds the membrane around the eyes. This is made from A&B two-part plumber's epoxy (available at carving-supply stores) rolled into a string. The area around the eye should be clean and free of dust before beginning this step.

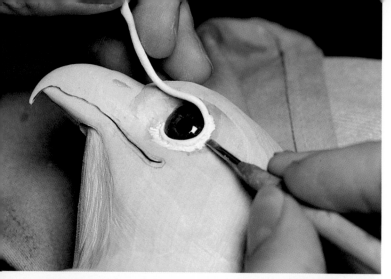

Floyd mixes equal parts of the water-soluble putty, kneads it until it becomes uniform, and rolls out a string about 1/16 inch in diameter. The string is pointed at one end. Floyd lays the tapered end on the inside of the eye, where the tear duct would be, and gently presses the epoxy into place.

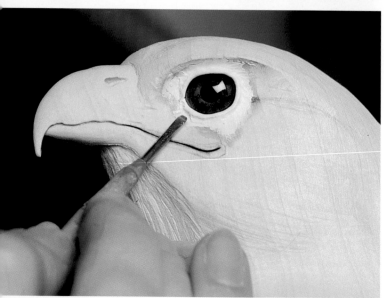

Floyd uses a piece of copper wire mounted in a handle to shape the membrane. The tip is moistened to prevent sticking. The outer edge of the putty is blended into the wood, but the inner part is not touched. Wetting the tool helps blend the putty into the wood.

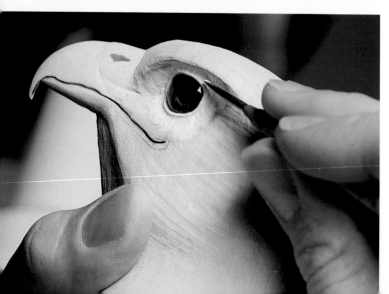

"This process gives life and personality to the bird," says Floyd. "You can make it look alert, serious, mean, whatever. It's a part of the process I really enjoy."

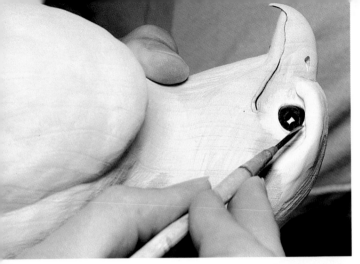

Floyd also adds a bit of the putty to the brow of the hawk to build it up. "I want a scowling, tough-guy look, and building up the brow helps accomplish this," he says. The putty sets up in about an hour and can then be sanded and textured just like wood.

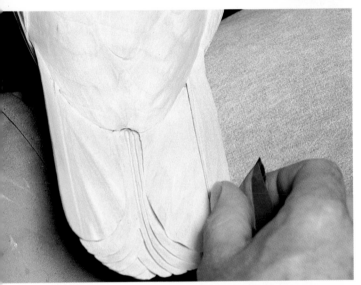

The final step in the carving process is burning each individual barb on each feather. It is a laborious, time-consuming process that, like sanding, greatly improves the final product. Floyd will begin under the tail and first gives the area a final sanding.

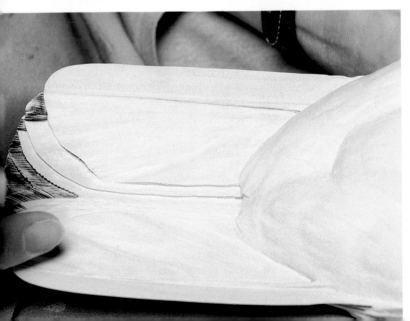

"Starting your texturing on the bottom of the tail, which is normally out of view, gives you a chance to establish your rhythm and spacing and timing," Floyd advises. "By the time you get to the top of the bird, you'll have the technique down."

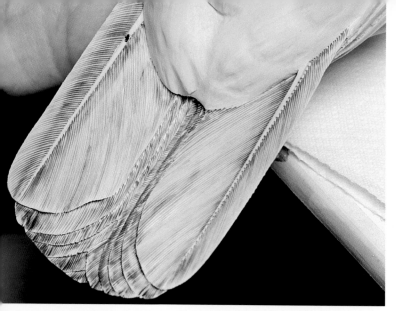

Texture lines are carved with a gentle curve, running from the shaft of the feather to the outer margin. Floyd uses two different burning tips and two different techniques. The spear point is used to carve the feather shafts, and a skew tip is used for burning the fine barbs. When burning barbs on large feathers, Floyd works from the shaft outward. With the small feathers of the upper back and head, he burns from the outside of the feather toward the shaft.

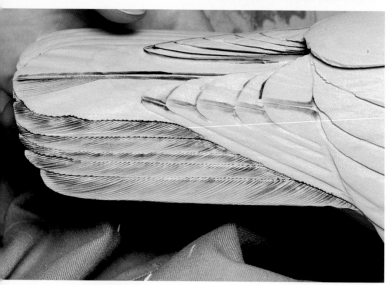

Floyd begins burning feather detail under the tail, then he moves to the top sides of the tail feathers.

Floyd works his way up the back of the bird, going from the tail feathers to the primaries and secondary flight feathers.

The burning pen can also be used to create some other subtle details that help give the illusion of softness and make the bird more realistic. Here Floyd adds a few splits to the tail feathers.

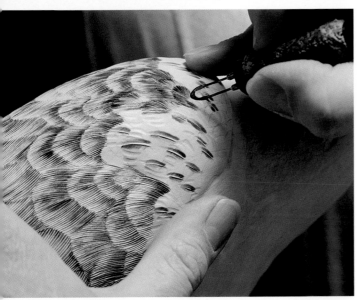

Burning is a time-consuming process that Floyd likens to playing music. "You have to warm up and run through the scales before you begin the piece," he says. "It takes a lot of practice, as well as good preparation, to get a good, tight burn."

The burned lines are applied over the carved texture lines Floyd added earlier with the burnishing tool in the high-speed grinder. The feather flow is established with tight, consistent burn lines.

Working his way up the bird, Floyd begins texturing the back and nape. Here he uses the spear tip to begin carving feather shafts.

As before, Floyd scribes two nearly parallel lines that come to a point at the tip of the feather. The ridge created by these two lines represents the shaft.

High up on the back, Floyd burns the feathers from the outer edge inward, which gives them a bit more flow and fullness.

This area shows the result of the two burning techniques. The larger feathers on the right have shafts and were burned from the shaft outward. The smaller ones were burned by moving the instrument from the edge of the feather inward.

For most feather burning, Floyd sets the instrument on medium heat. The higher the heat setting, the darker and deeper the burn.

When carving and shaping the head, you should be very aware of the direction of feather flow around the eyes and bill. Here, Floyd uses the sanding drum carefully to extend the eye grooves.

The sanding drum is applied to the head so that the lines it creates are consistent with the feather flow. Consult photographs, live birds, or mounted specimens, and study this area carefully to see the direction in which the feathers lie.

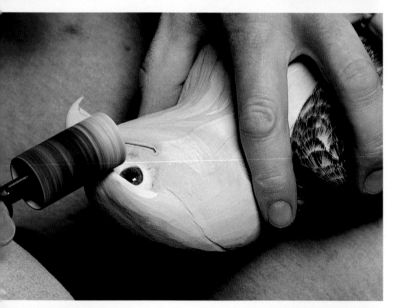

The brow area is sanded lightly where Floyd added the epoxy compound.

To make sure he carves texture lines that go with the feather flow, Floyd often will sketch these lines with pencil, feeling that it's better to spend time planning rather than correcting mistakes.

The high-speed grinder with the flame-tipped ruby stone is used to cut furrows along the pencil lines.

The lines at this stage appear to be overdone, but the edges will be softened later, and the effect will be that of facial muscles underlying groups of feathers.

Before the fine texturing is done, Floyd works a bit more on the shape of the neck, reducing it slightly.

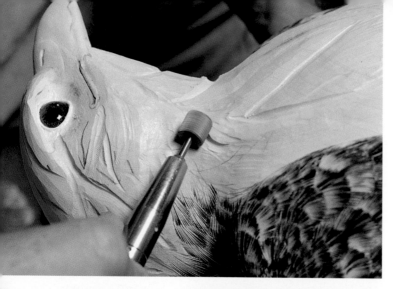

The stump cutter is used to soften the edges of the channels cut on the sides of the face.

Floyd sketches spear-shaped feathers on top of the head and uses the burnishing ball to carve them. The feathers on top of the head are not as rounded as those on the body of the hawk.

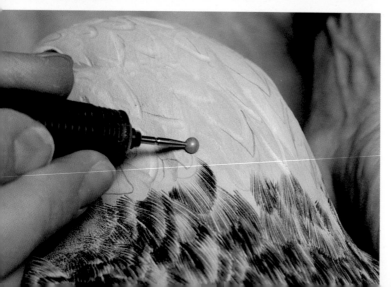

Floyd doesn't stone in each feather on the head; the carved lines represent groups or clumps of feathers.

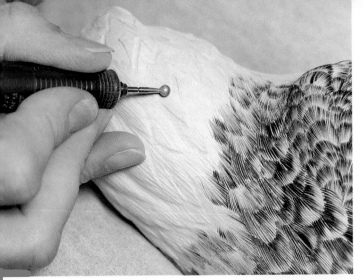

The goal here is to produce the illusion of layers of feathers that lie in a certain direction. The stoned lines represent the margins of the feather groups, and the lines establish the direction in which the feathers lie.

The carving process is similar to those used throughout this project. After a thorough sanding, the stone is used to carve lines in the surface of the wood, and then these lines are rounded off and made more subtle.

Floyd uses 150-grit sandpaper in the slotted mandrel on his Gesswein tool to round off the edges of the carved lines and make them less severe.

"At this stage, double check the area very closely to be sure that it's extremely well sanded," Floyd says. If so, the head is now ready to be burned.

Floyd burns the sides and top of the head and textures the throat area with the small cylinder. He begins at the nape and works his way up to the cere and eye region.

"I pay particular attention to burning the head," Floyd says. "You want a tight, clean burn here. The feathers around the head and eyes are a lot finer than the body feathers and flight feathers, so spend some extra time and burn as tight as you can."

Note here the combination of burned and stoned texture lines. The stone is generally used on the soft, fluffy feathers, such as those of the throat and belly.

To texture the breast, Floyd sands the area that was earlier stoned and redraws the individual feather groups. He begins with 150-grit sandpaper and progresses to 600-grit.

A burnishing ball is used to create the subtle ripples that add substantial fullness to the area.

This fullness is also very important in the tarsus, or "pants," of the bird. Floyd recommends slightly undercutting some of those feathers to accentuate the loose, jagged look around the ends of that feather group.

A small, white Arkansas cylinder is used to carve small lines that represent individual feather barbs.

The cylinder essentially does the same job as the burning tool, but the effect is softer and in keeping with the hairlike feathers of the breast and tarsus.

After the entire bird has been textured, Floyd carefully inspects all surfaces and touches up areas that need additional work. "Take your time," says Floyd. "It's difficult to go back and texture once the bird has been sealed for painting.

CHAPTER EIGHT

Painting and Putting It All Together

Painting the red-tailed hawk is a straightforward process. You first seal the surface and apply gesso to obtain a uniform painting surface, then add base tones of color, followed by final washes of color and detailing. Nothing to it.

Painting the bird really isn't difficult, Floyd insists. Just take things one step at a time.

The color palette is not extensive; the red-tail is a bird of earth colors, lots of burnt umber and burnt sienna. For painting this project, Floyd uses burnt umber, burnt sienna, ultramarine blue, yellow oxide, unbleached titanium, Payne's gray, lamp black, and white gesso. Flow Medium, a wetting agent, is used to ensure a smooth application of paint, and Pryme, an alcohol-based sealer, is applied before painting. A matte acrylic spray is used after painting.

The primary color of the hawk is a mixture of about 80 percent burnt umber and 20 percent ultramarine blue. This rich, dark color goes on the flight feathers, nape, and head, and it is used to paint the fleckings on the breast and belly.

The breast and belly are light, a mixture of raw sienna and burnt umber. The deep red tail of the hawk is created by mixing equal portions of burnt umber and burnt sienna.

Floyd spends a great deal of time doing detail work with this bird, paying particular attention to the area around the eyes and beak. Lamp black is used for the tiny rictal bristles, gesso creates highlights around the yellow cere, and numerous washes of gesso and Payne's gray, followed by a wash of straight Payne's gray give the beak a realistic leathery quality.

The hawk can be painted in its entirety with conventional brushes, or an airbrush can be substituted for some of the tasks. Floyd uses the airbrush to put on some of the preliminary base colors and to paint the markings on the flight feathers. The machine is quicker than the hand in these steps, and it provides nice, soft edge. If you don't have an airbrush, the same effect can be obtained with a soft sable brush.

Before he begins painting, Floyd stabilizes the bird, fastening it to a heavy, temporary base by inserting a threaded steel rod into its belly. From this point on, he tries to avoid touching the hawk, because even freshly washed hands can transfer unwanted oils onto the wood. When the painting is complete, Floyd will remove the rod and fill the hole with A&B epoxy putty, touching up with paint to conceal the filling.

Floyd begins the painting process by sealing the wood with Pryme, and then he applies three thin coats of gesso to create a consistent painting surface. Next come the base tones, such as the browns that cover the wings. Floyd then builds up final colors through a series of washes and adds details such as bristles and feather splits.

Before painting, Floyd seals the wood by applying two coats of Pryme, an alcohol-based sanding sealer made by the Fabulon company.

Gesso, mixed with water and a small amount of Flow Medium, is applied with a 1-inch oval wash brush. The goal is consistent coverage, because the gesso forms the foundation for the colors applied later.

Floyd begins by base toning the wings with brown, a mix of 80 percent burnt umber and 20 percent ultramarine blue. Floyd uses an airbrush for this step, but a large brush could be used.

The primary flight feathers are darkened with the brown, and then the tail is painted with a mixture of 70 percent burnt sienna and 30 percent burnt umber. The white tip of the tail, known as the terminal band, is not painted, as the white gesso shows from underneath.

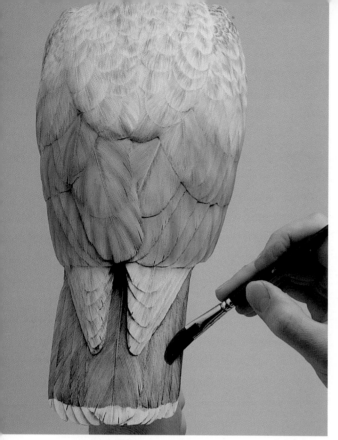

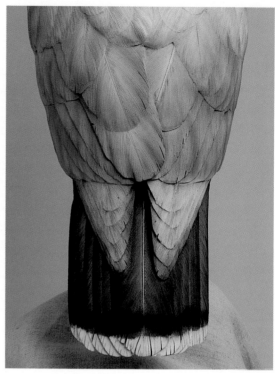

Using a 1/2-inch oval wash brush, Floyd builds up the intensity of the color of the tail by adding successive thin washes of the burnt sienna and burnt umber mixture. A touch of Jo Sonja Flow Medium is added to make the paint flow easily into the carved detail. It's important to build up the intensity of the color slowly, through a series of thin washes. Avoid the temptation to save time by putting on the paint too thickly, and dry each coat thoroughly before adding the next.

After building up the color of the tail, Floyd finishes the area by adding a black subterminal band, shown above. This is a 50-50 mix of ultramarine blue and burnt umber. It can be applied by brush or airbrush.

The dark bars of the tertial, secondary, and secondary covert feathers are painted with an airbrush loaded with a mix of 70 percent burnt umber and 30 percent ultramarine blue.

The back is completed, with the exception of the nape and scapular feathers. The airbrush provides a soft edge, and the color can be built up gradually.

This side view shows the patterns used on the upper median covert feathers and shoulder and wrist area. The feathers are darkened near the center and left lighter at the edges. The cere has been give a base coat of yellow, which is yellow oxide with a touch of burnt sienna.

The wing is darkened by adding thin washes of the 80-20 mix of burnt umber and ultramarine blue, this time applied with the brush. This step brings the values of the light and dark areas closer together.

Floyd uses an 8408 series Rafael brush to add the thin white edges to the large flight feathers. The paint is unbleached titanium to which a small amount of Flow Medium is added.

The same technique is used on the secondary feathers. The line should be thin and not call attention to itself.

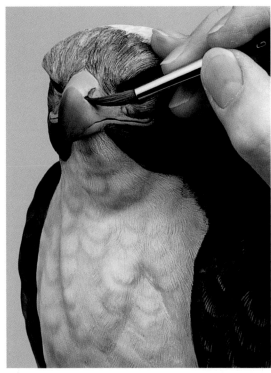

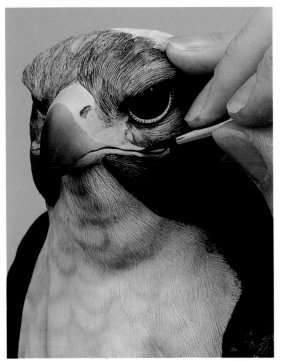

Floyd now puts on the base tone color of the beak, which is a mix of 70 percent white gesso and 30 percent Payne's gray. He uses an 8408 series brush and adds Flow Medium to the color to make it go on smoothly. As on the tail feathers, the color is built up gradually through a series of thin washes.

Straight Payne's gray is used for the final washes. The color is diluted with water, and more washes are applied near the tip to make this area darker. A light wash of yellow is also applied to the edge of the cere.

Floyd darkens the separation between the upper and lower mandibles, giving it definition.

Further detailing is done around the eye, painting in the black whiskers and dots on the eyelids.

Additional wash coats of straight burnt umber are applied to the lower jaw to darken it and create a shadow.

Wash coats of the same color are applied over the top edge of the cere to darken it and soften the edge.

Straight gesso is brushed onto the areas in front of the eyes.

A number 2 brush is used to paint in the small rictal bristles that spiral outward from in front of the eye. Straight lamp black is used here. Floyd also adds detail where the wings fold over the sides of the breast, painting a few lines that suggest splits and breaks where these two feather groups meet.

This side profile shows the completed wing, tail, and face.

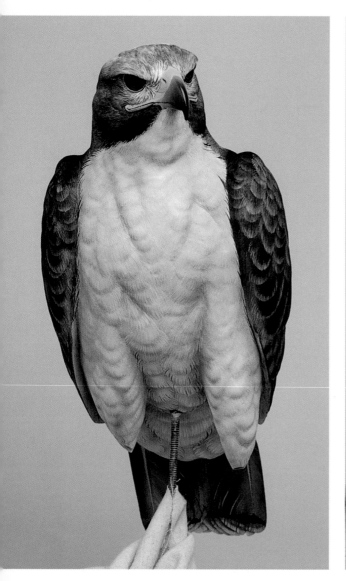
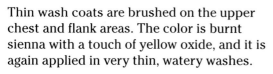

Thin wash coats are brushed on the upper chest and flank areas. The color is burnt sienna with a touch of yellow oxide, and it is again applied in very thin, watery washes.

The scapular feathers, nape, and back of the head have been painted with the mix of 70 percent burnt umber and 30 percent ultramarine blue.

The head is completed. Note the detail around the eyes, bill, and cere. Good reference material is essential in doing a realistic and accurate job of painting.

This front view shows further facial detail. The white detail above the cere is straight gesso, applied with a small brush.

A final step is the addition of the markings that constitute the diagnostic belly band of the hawk. This series of markings is painted with the mix used earlier on the wings, 70 percent burnt umber and 30 percent ultramarine blue.

Fleckings are applied to the sides of the breast all the way up to the neck. Note how the size and shape of the marks vary. This completes the painting process. Floyd now seals the paint with a thin mist of matte acrylic spray, which protects the surface and adds a subtle sheen.

Adding the Feet and Legs

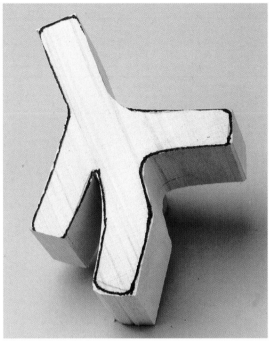

Floyd uses a cardboard pattern that is slightly larger than the actual foot. He says, "Be careful when using feet from dead birds—especially raptors—as reference. When the leg and toes dry out, they shrink considerably."

Floyd draws the pattern onto a 1 1/2″ thick block of tupelo and then uses a bandsaw to rough out the foot.

He draws a centerline on the top of each toe and begins rounding and shaping.

PHOTOS BY TAD MERRICK (THROUGH PAGE 86)

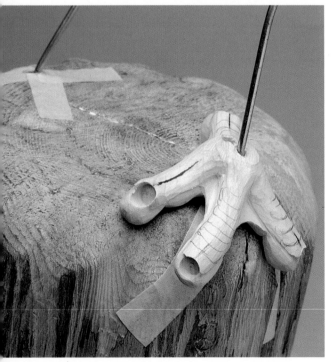

Floyd uses a large carbide round ball to begin hollowing out the underside of the foot.

Strips of masking tape help to define foot position. For strength and support, a brass rod is inserted through the foot and into the base. [Note: Floyd carved the feet in this series of photos for a later project, which is why the base differs from the one pictured at the end of chapter 8. The techniques, however, are the same, and can be used to create any foot position.]

Floyd continues to add definition to the feet and toes, carving in the scales and using a 1/4-inch diamond cylinder on a Gesswein tool to hollow out sockets for the talons. Throughout the process, he checks the shape and curvature of the toes to ensure that they will fit the base.

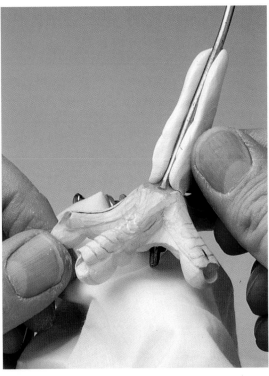

The talons are made by rolling and shaping Super Sculpey modeling clay, available from the Polyform Products Company. Baked at 300°F for 20 minutes, the talons harden to the consistency of hard plastic.

A&B two-part plumber's epoxy is rolled out and wrapped around the central leg shaft. After an hour, when the putty has begun to harden, Floyd uses a copper wire mounted in a handle (see page 58) to define the major scales. When the putty is completely dry, he adds fine detail with a small pointed ruby carver.

Floyd glues in the talons and seals the entire foot with two coats of Pryme. When the sealer is thoroughly dry, he uses a 1/2-inch oval wash brush to apply gesso to the entire foot and leg.

85

The foot and leg are painted with a 50-50 mixture of yellow oxide and unbleached titanium.

Floyd paints the talons with a 50-50 mixture of ultramarine blue and burnt umber. He highlights the tops of the scales with a lighter mixture of the foot and leg color.

To add detail, Floyd uses a thin, watery wash of burnt sienna mixed with a touch of raw umber. He allows the pigments to settle into the nooks and crannies of the foot, then mists the entire foot with acrylic matte medium.

To join the legs to the body, Floyd uses five-minute epoxy resin to glue the leg shaft into its corresponding socket, blending the two parts with A&B epoxy putty. When the putty is thoroughly dry, Floyd uses a 1/8-inch square-end diamond cylinder to stone in the texture of the feathers as they overlap the leg shafts, and he paints the remaining feathers.

The Finished Carving

Satisfied with his creation, Floyd comments on the hawk:

"You can see how the texturing and painting work together to create a pleasing feather flow throughout the head and body. I also like the intensity in this hawk's face."

"The feet and toes should grasp the branch realistically. A too-tight grip will look unnatural."

"You can take some artistic license with the layout of the streaks and markings on the chest and belly. Strive to accentuate flow without overcrowding any one area."

"Small areas can be so important. Look at the overlay of upper chest feathers onto the shoulder, here. Transition areas should look dynamic, yet natural."

"Here you can see the careful layout of the upper wing region, which many carvers find confusing. Resolving the feather flow can be tricky, but careful study of reference material can help."

"All the burn lines are slightly curved to accentuate the roundness of the individual feathers."

"The feathers of the head get tighter and more spear pointed as they flow toward the bill."

"The major flight feathers have interesting shapes and contrast nicely when properly arranged."

"Occasional splits and breaks can add a great deal of personality to feathers."